National Parks

2024

WEEKLY PLANNER

July 2023–December 2024

ROCK
POINT

2024 Year at a Glance

JANUARY

S	M	T	W	T	F	S
	1	2	3	4	5	6
7	8	9	10	11	12	13
14	15	16	17	18	19	20
21	22	23	24	25	26	27
28	29	30	31			

FEBRUARY

S	M	T	W	T	F	S
				1	2	3
4	5	6	7	8	9	10
11	12	13	14	15	16	17
18	19	20	21	22	23	24
25	26	27	28	29		

MARCH

S	M	T	W	T	F	S
					1	2
3	4	5	6	7	8	9
10	11	12	13	14	15	16
17	18	19	20	21	22	23
24	25	26	27	28	29	30
31						

APRIL

S	M	T	W	T	F	S
	1	2	3	4	5	6
7	8	9	10	11	12	13
14	15	16	17	18	19	20
21	22	23	24	25	26	27
28	29	30				

MAY

S	M	T	W	T	F	S
			1	2	3	4
5	6	7	8	9	10	11
12	13	14	15	16	17	18
19	20	21	22	23	24	25
26	27	28	29	30	31	

JUNE

S	M	T	W	T	F	S
						1
2	3	4	5	6	7	8
9	10	11	12	13	14	15
16	17	18	19	20	21	22
23	24	25	26	27	28	29
30						

JULY

S	M	T	W	T	F	S
	1	2	3	4	5	6
7	8	9	10	11	12	13
14	15	16	17	18	19	20
21	22	23	24	25	26	27
28	29	30	31			

AUGUST

S	M	T	W	T	F	S
				1	2	3
4	5	6	7	8	9	10
11	12	13	14	15	16	17
18	19	20	21	22	23	24
25	26	27	28	29	30	31

SEPTEMBER

S	M	T	W	T	F	S
1	2	3	4	5	6	7
8	9	10	11	12	13	14
15	16	17	18	19	20	21
22	23	24	25	26	27	28
29	30					

OCTOBER

S	M	T	W	T	F	S
		1	2	3	4	5
6	7	8	9	10	11	12
13	14	15	16	17	18	19
20	21	22	23	24	25	26
27	28	29	30	31		

NOVEMBER

S	M	T	W	T	F	S
					1	2
3	4	5	6	7	8	9
10	11	12	13	14	15	16
17	18	19	20	21	22	23
24	25	26	27	28	29	30

DECEMBER

S	M	T	W	T	F	S
1	2	3	4	5	6	7
8	9	10	11	12	13	14
15	16	17	18	19	20	21
22	23	24	25	26	27	28
29	30	31				

2025 Year at a Glance

JANUARY

S	M	T	W	T	F	S
			1	2	3	4
5	6	7	8	9	10	11
12	13	14	15	16	17	18
19	20	21	22	23	24	25
26	27	28	29	30	31	

FEBRUARY

S	M	T	W	T	F	S
						1
2	3	4	5	6	7	8
9	10	11	12	13	14	15
16	17	18	19	20	21	22
23	24	25	26	27	28	

MARCH

S	M	T	W	T	F	S
						1
2	3	4	5	6	7	8
9	10	11	12	13	14	15
16	17	18	19	20	21	22
23	24	25	26	27	28	29
30	31					

APRIL

S	M	T	W	T	F	S
		1	2	3	4	5
6	7	8	9	10	11	12
13	14	15	16	17	18	19
20	21	22	23	24	25	26
27	28	29	30			

MAY

S	M	T	W	T	F	S
				1	2	3
4	5	6	7	8	9	10
11	12	13	14	15	16	17
18	19	20	21	22	23	24
25	26	27	28	29	30	31

JUNE

S	M	T	W	T	F	S
1	2	3	4	5	6	7
8	9	10	11	12	13	14
15	16	17	18	19	20	21
22	23	24	25	26	27	28
29	30					

JULY

S	M	T	W	T	F	S
		1	2	3	4	5
6	7	8	9	10	11	12
13	14	15	16	17	18	19
20	21	22	23	24	25	26
27	28	29	30	31		

AUGUST

S	M	T	W	T	F	S
					1	2
3	4	5	6	7	8	9
10	11	12	13	14	15	16
17	18	19	20	21	22	23
24	25	26	27	28	29	30
31						

SEPTEMBER

S	M	T	W	T	F	S
	1	2	3	4	5	6
7	8	9	10	11	12	13
14	15	16	17	18	19	20
21	22	23	24	25	26	27
28	29	30				

OCTOBER

S	M	T	W	T	F	S
			1	2	3	4
5	6	7	8	9	10	11
12	13	14	15	16	17	18
19	20	21	22	23	24	25
26	27	28	29	30	31	

NOVEMBER

S	M	T	W	T	F	S
						1
2	3	4	5	6	7	8
9	10	11	12	13	14	15
16	17	18	19	20	21	22
23	24	25	26	27	28	29
30						

DECEMBER

S	M	T	W	T	F	S
	1	2	3	4	5	6
7	8	9	10	11	12	13
14	15	16	17	18	19	20
21	22	23	24	25	26	27
28	29	30	31			

JULY
Glacier National Park

Declared a national park in 1910 by President Taft, Glacier National Park in northwest Montana preserves 1 million acres of breathtaking glacier-carved peaks and valleys, pristine aquamarine lakes, yawning alpine meadows, and an abundance of vegetation and wildlife. A nature-lover's utopia, this stunning park has endless recreational opportunities with over 700 miles of trails for hiking and biking, forest bathing, rafting, and camping. In this ancient park, observe glaciers so powerful they cut through stone, creating majestic mountain peaks that reach for the sky to form the formidable Rocky Mountains. Picnic in fields of wildflowers bursting with color, float

down a sleepy river, or flex your adventure muscles and raft lively rapids. While you explore, keep your eyes peeled for sightings of bears, elk, deer, moose, and myriad of native birds. The park is home to 26 glaciers, down from 150 since the year 1850 due to climate change, a number that continues to shrink in rapid decline. A leader in understanding, educating, and taking action on environmental damage from climate change, Glacier National Park's visitor centers and ranger stations are solar powered, feature micro-hydroelectric powerplants, enforces strong policy on recycling, discourages idling, and encourages the use of reusable and recyclable gear.

July 2023

NOTES	SUNDAY	MONDAY	TUESDAY
	2 ○	3	4
			INDEPENDENCE DAY (US)
	9 ◗	10	11
	16 ●	17	18
	23	24 ◖	25
	30	31	

JULY 2023

WEDNESDAY	THURSDAY	FRIDAY	SATURDAY
			1 CANADA DAY (CAN)
5	6	7	8
12	13	14	15
19	20	21	22
26	27	28	29

GLACIER NATIONAL PARK

LOCATION: Northwestern Montana, on the Canada–United States border

CLIMATE: Rainfall averages 23 inches a year, while the lowlands of the west side receive about 30 inches of precipitation on average. Temperatures can reach upwards of 90°F in the summer with chilly nights, and below-freezing temperatures in the winter months.

BEST TIME TO VISIT: Late June through September

BIODIVERSITY: 24 varieties of fish, 71 species of mammals, 276 documented birds, and 1,990 types of plants and trees

COMMON WILDLIFE: Grizzly and black bears, mountain goats, moose, big horn sheep, coyotes, wolves, beavers, pika, mountain lions, elk, white-tailed deer, beavers, otters, porcupines

RECREATION: Over 730 miles of hiking and biking trails, park and backcountry camping, ranger-led programs and tours, fishing, boating, river floating and whitewater rafting, cross-country skiing, star gazing

NOTABLE ATTRACTIONS: Lake McDonald, Going-to-the-Sun Road, Avalanche Lake, Saint Mary Lake, Logan Pass Visitor Center, Huckleberry Lookout, Glacier Park Lodge

MONDAY (JUNE)

26

TUESDAY (JUNE)

27

WEDNESDAY (JUNE)

28

THURSDAY (JUNE)

29

FRIDAY (JUNE)

30

SATURDAY CANADA DAY (CAN)

1

SUNDAY

2

JULY 2023

MONDAY ●

3

TUESDAY INDEPENDENCE DAY (US)

4

WEDNESDAY

5

THURSDAY

6

FRIDAY

7

SATURDAY

8

SUNDAY

9

The mountain goat is the symbol of Glacier, so keep your eyes open for these majestic creatures.

July 2023

MONDAY ☽

10

TUESDAY

11

WEDNESDAY

12

THURSDAY

13

FRIDAY

14

SATURDAY

15

SUNDAY

16

Take a tour of the park on a Jammer, a vintage and historic red tour bus used to reduce traffic.

July 2023

MONDAY ●   17

TUESDAY   18

WEDNESDAY   19

THURSDAY   20

FRIDAY 21

SATURDAY 22

SUNDAY 23

Going-to-the-Sun Road is featured in the opening shot of the film The Shining.

July 2023

MONDAY — **24**

TUESDAY ◖ — **25**

WEDNESDAY — **26**

THURSDAY — **27**

FRIDAY

28

SATURDAY

29

SUNDAY

30

For a scenic route to the park, take Amtrak's Empire Builder train straight to the entrance.

AUGUST
Yellowstone National Park

Ready to explore one of the most popular and exciting natural landscapes in the United States? Yellowstone covers the northwest corner of Wyoming, parts of Montana, and Idaho. Yellowstone was declared the first national park in the United States by Ulysses S. Grant in 1872. The park's many lakes, canyons, rivers, and mountains occupy some of the highest elevations in the United States. It's home to the world's most famous geyser, Old Faithful, which erupts approximately every hour and thirty minutes. It's also home to 500 to 700 active geysers, as well as hot springs, mudpots, and fumaroles. Visit the colorful Morning Glory pool and the Grand Prismatic Spring with dramatic yellow and teal tones, the volatile Grotto Geyser, or the enchanting Fairy Falls—this park is filled to the brim with beauty. It even has its very own Grand Canyon featuring

death-defying waterfalls and sweeping vistas. Yellowstone's drama is owed to being centered over a super volcano called the Yellowstone Caldera, a dormant volcano that fuels its various geothermal attractions. Yellowstone is also home to an extensive museum collection documenting travel to and through the park, as well as archives, a research library, an archeology lab, and herbarium. The archive maintains the historical records of both the park itself and the National Parks Service at large, in cooperation with the Native American populations that have occupied the region for over ten thousand years. This UNESCO World Heritage site is also home to a wide variety of animals—grizzly bears, gray wolves, and the country's largest, oldest, free-ranging American Bison herd. Yellowstone is world-renowned for housing herds of bison, so be sure to watch for these awe-inspiring creatures.

AUGUST 2023

NOTES	SUNDAY	MONDAY	TUESDAY
			○ 1
	6	7 ☽	8
		SUMMER BANK HOLIDAY (UK-SCT)	
	13	14	15
	20	21	22
	27	28	29
		SUMMER BANK HOLIDAY (UK-ENG / NIR / WAL)	

AUGUST 2023

WEDNESDAY	THURSDAY	FRIDAY	SATURDAY
2	3	4	5
9	10	11	12
● 16	17	18	19
23 ☾	24	25	26
○ 30	31		

YELLOWSTONE NATIONAL PARK

LOCATION: Wyoming, Montana, and Idaho

CLIMATE: The park receives on average 20 inches of rainfall a year. Temperatures can reach upwards of 90°F in the summer and lows of around 30°F, while winter months drop below freezing.

BEST TIME TO VISIT: April through October

BIODIVERSITY: 300 species of birds, and 16 species of fish, five species of amphibians, six species of reptiles, and over 60 species of mammals

COMMON WILDLIFE: American Bison, bear, mountain lions and bobcats, bighorn sheep, moose and elk, gray wolf, red fox, mountain goats, multiple species of deer, lynx, coyotes

RECREATION: Hiking, biking, horse riding, skiing and snowshoeing, camping, ranger-led programs and tours, wildlife tours and observation, swimming and soaking pool, rafting and paddling

NOTABLE ATTRACTIONS: Grand Loop, Old Faithful, Upper Geyser Basin, Morning Glory Pool, the Grand Prismatic Spring, Mammoth Hot Springs and Minerva Terrace, Hayden and Lamar Valleys, Specimen Ridge, the Grand Canyon of Yellowstone, Eagle Mountain, Mount Washburn

MONDAY (JULY) 31

TUESDAY ◯ 1

WEDNESDAY 2

THURSDAY 3

FRIDAY 4

SATURDAY 5

SUNDAY 6

August 2023

MONDAY SUMMER BANK HOLIDAY (UK-SCT) 7

TUESDAY ☽ 8

WEDNESDAY 9

THURSDAY 10

FRIDAY

11

SATURDAY

12

SUNDAY

13

Yellowstone contains half of the world's geothermal features.

August 2023

MONDAY 14

TUESDAY 15

WEDNESDAY ● 16

THURSDAY 17

FRIDAY

18

SATURDAY

19

SUNDAY

20

The park's most famous geyser is Old Faithful, which got its name for the equal time between eruptions—but which are getting more inconsistent over time.

AUGUST 2023

MONDAY 21

TUESDAY 22

WEDNESDAY 23

THURSDAY 24

FRIDAY 25

SATURDAY 26

SUNDAY 27

While driving the scenic roads surrounding Yellowstone, watch for bison—they roam freely across the roads.

SEPTEMBER

Great Smoky Mountains National Park

S trike out into the heart of the southern Appalachian Mountains where the Great Smoky Mountains National Park contains enormous swaths of pre-colonial old-growth forest. This beautiful, lush landscape features 70 miles of the Appalachian trail and serves almost twice the number of visitors as the Grand Canyon. A network of old-growth forests, ancient mountains, and human history, this is America's most visited national park. Packed with opportunities to hike, camp, fish, bike, and otherwise explore the expanses of the stunning landscape, it has a variety of historical attractions, including preserved buildings and self-guided tours of the historical areas, peaks, and waterfalls. This park is full of magical moments, from the splendor of firefly displays to a world-recognized preserve of wildflower diversity with over 1,500 kinds of flowering plants. Opportunities to watch wildlife abound, including a newly introduced population of elk.

Drive through Newfound Gap, the park's lowest drivable pass, or tour the Roaring Fork Motor train for stunning vistas, like Rainbow and Grotto Falls, without the hike.

The Smoky Mountains also contain some of the largest preserves of pre-colonial native forests, and archaeological evidence dating back as far as 8,000 years, making it a place of rich history for both humans and our greater ecological community. You can also learn about more modern human relationships to this land at the Mountain Farm Museum and other educational sites. Visit in the fall for spectacular colors in the turning leaves and misty mountain views while climbing Clingmans Dome or driving through Cades Cove to spot bears. When you're done with your visit, make sure to take the famous Blue Ridge Parkway on your way out.

SEPTEMBER 2023

NOTES	SUNDAY	MONDAY	TUESDAY
	3	**4**	**5**
	FATHER'S DAY (AUS / NZ)	LABOR DAY (US) LABOUR DAY (CAN)	
	10	**11**	**12**
	GRANDPARENTS' DAY (US)	PATRIOT DAY (US)	
	17	**18**	**19**
	24	**25**	**26**
	YOM KIPPUR (BEGINS AT SUNDOWN)		

SEPTEMBER 2023

WEDNESDAY	THURSDAY	FRIDAY	SATURDAY
		1	2
6	7	8	9
13	14	15 **ROSH HASHANAH (BEGINS AT SUNDOWN)** **FIRST DAY OF NATIONAL HISPANIC HERITAGE MONTH**	16
20	21	22	23 **FALL EQUINOX**
27	28	29 **SUKKOT (BEGINS AT SUNDOWN)**	30

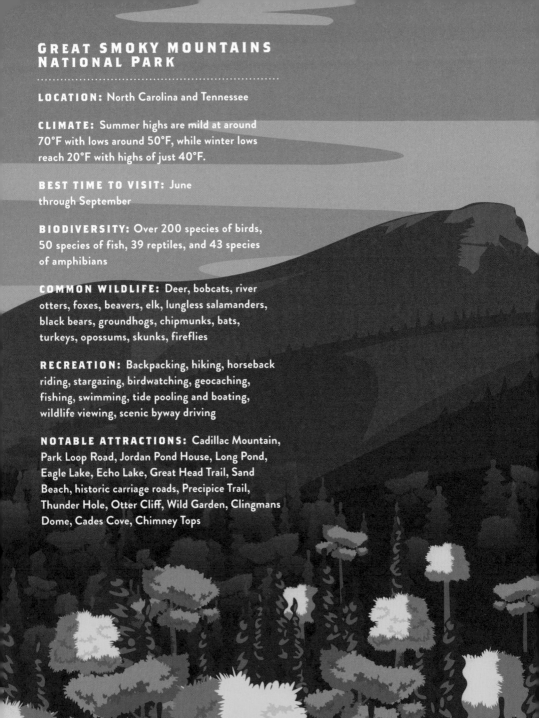

GREAT SMOKY MOUNTAINS NATIONAL PARK

LOCATION: North Carolina and Tennessee

CLIMATE: Summer highs are mild at around 70°F with lows around 50°F, while winter lows reach 20°F with highs of just 40°F.

BEST TIME TO VISIT: June through September

BIODIVERSITY: Over 200 species of birds, 50 species of fish, 39 reptiles, and 43 species of amphibians

COMMON WILDLIFE: Deer, bobcats, river otters, foxes, beavers, elk, lungless salamanders, black bears, groundhogs, chipmunks, bats, turkeys, opossums, skunks, fireflies

RECREATION: Backpacking, hiking, horseback riding, stargazing, birdwatching, geocaching, fishing, swimming, tide pooling and boating, wildlife viewing, scenic byway driving

NOTABLE ATTRACTIONS: Cadillac Mountain, Park Loop Road, Jordan Pond House, Long Pond, Eagle Lake, Echo Lake, Great Head Trail, Sand Beach, historic carriage roads, Precipice Trail, Thunder Hole, Otter Cliff, Wild Garden, Clingmans Dome, Cades Cove, Chimney Tops

MONDAY (AUGUST) SUMMER BANK HOLIDAY (UK-ENG / NIR / WAL)

28

TUESDAY (AUGUST)

29

WEDNESDAY (AUGUST) ○

30

THURSDAY (AUGUST)

31

FRIDAY

1

SATURDAY

2

SUNDAY FATHER'S DAY (AUS / NZ)

3

September 2023

MONDAY LABOR DAY (US) / LABOUR DAY (CAN)

4

TUESDAY

5

WEDNESDAY)

6

THURSDAY

7

FRIDAY

8

SATURDAY

9

SUNDAY GRANDPARENTS' DAY (US)

10

There is no entrance fee to explore Great Smoky, so what's stopping you?

September 2023

MONDAY PATRIOT DAY (US)

11

TUESDAY

12

WEDNESDAY

13

THURSDAY ●

14

FRIDAY ROSH HASHANAH (BEGINS AT SUNDOWN) /
FIRST DAY OF NATIONAL HISPANIC HERITAGE MONTH

15

SATURDAY

16

SUNDAY

17

With more than 30 species of salamanders, Great
Smoky is lovingly referred to as the Salamander
Capital of the World.

September 2023

MONDAY

18

TUESDAY

19

WEDNESDAY

20

THURSDAY

21

FRIDAY ◐

22

SATURDAY FALL EQUINOX

23

SUNDAY YOM KIPPUR (BEGINS AT SUNDOWN)

24

The Smoky Mountains are estimated to be between 200 and 300 million years old.

OCTOBER

Kenai Fjords National Park

Acrobat illustrator? — First Right of first refusal 'Contract?'

An icy wonderland that hosts a wealth of opportunities for adventure, Kenai Fjords National Park is most known for its outflowing glaciers and attendant coastal fjords and islands, creating the most beautiful park north of the lower 48. Situated in Alaska on the Harding Icefield, it contains some of the largest ice fields in the United States. It has been carved and shaped by the movements of glaciers as they travel from the mountainside to the coast, creating breathtaking fjords, a name for glacial valleys submerged below sea level. You can even explore the Exit Glacier, which visitors can drive right up to. Its unique formations ensure that the park has only one road in and out, and the majority of the impenetratable wilderness of the park is accessible by boat, airplane, and hiking. Its rich biosphere is home to a variety of endangered marine mammals and

Content 10/4 (Cont from calendar)
* * outcomes ? strong focus on members
   1) Local 2) Trusted partner 3) Committed to
                                    members
* Ryan Smith SP/Teams
   - setting -files - open preference to Desktop app.
   - Graphics - Tile view
   - Proposal Development + tools = Assignment
                                  = Cons Strway √ list
                                  = KS Brand guideline
                                         (style guide)
                                  = Program Catalogue
                                  = data parade

birds attuned to the long winters and endless summer days of Alaska. Time your travel carefully—about 50 percent of the park is covered in ice, and the Icefield gets almost 60 feet of snow a year!

Established by President Jimmy Carter in 1978, the park protects the unique geography of the ice field and its deeply scored coastline. The park is filled with wildlife, including brown and black bears, sea otters and harbor seals, humpback and killer whales, and moose. Its complicated history includes both Indigenous and colonial settlements, as well as gold mining, logging, and subsistence rights of local populations. Now Kenai Fjords is a popular destination for large cruise ships and guided tours given by both park rangers and private companies. This remote and majestic park offers unparalleled views of a unique landscape shaped by geological history, and is ever evolving, continuing to shift and change each year.

October 2023

NOTES	SUNDAY	MONDAY	TUESDAY
		1	2	3
			LABOUR DAY (AUS-ACT / NSW / SA)	
	8	9	10
		INDIGENOUS PEOPLES' DAY (US) **COLUMBUS DAY (US)** **THANKSGIVING DAY (CAN)**	
	15	16	17
	22	23	24
			LABOUR DAY (NZ)	
	29	30	31
			HALLOWEEN

October 2023

WEDNESDAY	THURSDAY	FRIDAY	SATURDAY
4	5 ☽	6	7
			SIMCHAT TORAH (BEGINS AT SUNDOWN)
11	12	13 ●	14
18	19	20 ◐	21
25	26	27 ○	28

Kenai Fjords National Park

LOCATION: Alaska

CLIMATE: Temperatures in the park vary widely by season, reaching highs of only 20°F in the winter and highs of 60°F in the summer months, with average temperatures between 20°F and 50°F year-round.

BEST TIME TO VISIT: June through August

BIODIVERSITY: 200 species of birds, as well as a variety of endangered species including humpback whales, sei, and gray whales, along with the Steller sea lion

COMMON WILDLIFE: Orcas, black oystercatchers, a variety of puffins, and bald eagles Watch for bears!

RECREATION: Boat tours, fishing, kayaking, wildlife cruises and air charters for sightseeing, as well as limited ice climbing, hiking, backpacking, and camping based on seasonal accessibility

NOTABLE ATTRACTIONS: Harding Icefield, Truuli Peak, Exit Glacier, Glacier Overlook Trail, Glacier View Loop, Exit Glacier Road

September/October

MONDAY (SEPTEMBER)

25

TUESDAY (SEPTEMBER)

26

WEDNESDAY (SEPTEMBER)

27

THURSDAY (SEPTEMBER)

28

FRIDAY (SEPTEMBER) SUKKOT (BEGINS AT SUNDOWN) ○

29

SATURDAY (SEPTEMBER)

30

SUNDAY

1

OCTOBER 2023

MONDAY LABOUR DAY (AUS-ACT / NSW / SA)   **2**

TUESDAY   **3**

WEDNESDAY   **4**

Centre → 8-930

HCBS 120 risk pmt

10/17 - Strategy Sessions

PDC 1030-

* 2013 start of operations
* NCQA → HCBS & SDOH
* Not a Medicaid expansion state
* 143 k medicaid total
* 520,000 Medicaid & CHP in KS
* RedTeam 11/7 - 10/23
  war room 12/11-14
  - production 12/18 start
* cm for kids w/ sud & foster care
  - in person visits requirements
  - not mtg ratios currently (evaluate monthly)

THURSDAY   **5**

Agenda: 1) questions? unclear language
2) what does the ? means
3) outline w/in each section
4) data points decisions needed that haven't been figured out?

outstanding bus. decisions

5) data points

FRIDAY ◗

6

SATURDAY SIMCHAT TORAH (BEGINS AT SUNDOWN)

7

SUNDAY

8

A whopping 50 percent of Kenai Fjords' terrain is covered in ice.

OCTOBER 2023

MONDAY INDIGENOUS PEOPLES' DAY (US) / COLUMBUS DAY (US) / THANKSGIVING DAY (CAN)

9

TUESDAY

10

WEDNESDAY

11

THURSDAY

12

FRIDAY 13

SATURDAY ● 14

SUNDAY 15

Take a zip line or walk a suspension bridge to get a bird's-eye view of the park from above.

October 2023

MONDAY 16

TUESDAY 17

WEDNESDAY 18

THURSDAY 19

FRIDAY

20

SATURDAY ☽

21

SUNDAY

22

Visit the quaint town of Seward for a taste of the local food, shops, breweries, and lodging options.

October 2023

MONDAY LABOUR DAY (NZ)

23

TUESDAY

24

WEDNESDAY

25

THURSDAY

26

FRIDAY

27

SATURDAY ○

28

SUNDAY

29

Take a boat tour to view aquatic wildlife: whales and otters and seals, oh my!

November
Zion National Park

With its enormous sandstone cliffs that tower over the horizon, Mount Zion was the first national park in Utah. Its dramatic landscape, colors, and rich terrain capture the imagination, with hikes along breathtaking sheer cliffs at Angels Landing and impressive outlooks that allow you to embrace the expansive horizon. The famous slot canyons plunge deep and narrow with colorful walls that provide dramatic photographic opportunities as well as hikes. This unforgettable park was established in 1919 by President Woodrow Wilson. Indigenous Peoples have lived here for over 8,000 years, and its eroded canyons and cliffs reveal 150 million years of history. Over 85 percent of the park is designated as wilderness areas, and the park exists specifically to preserve the dramatic and rich landscape of the brilliant sandstone canyons. Its evocatively named peaks include the Sundial, the Witch Head, Broken Tooth, the Great White Throne, the Watchman,

and the Altar of Sacrifice. It also features one of the world's most extended natural arches, Kolob Arch. While this desert park is known for its remarkable sandstone formations, it also features the Emerald Pools, a series of oases with lush vegetation, waterfalls, and monoliths for hikers to admire. The Virgin River and its tributaries wind through the park, creating gorges, gullies, and canyons that mold the landscape to create cascading waterfalls. The finger canyons of Kolob and the cool river canyons of the Narrows are also popular hikes with the visitors who arrive year-round, though some adventures, like The Subway—a small slot canyon—require your swimsuit. Canyoneering and rock climbing are unique offerings available for a more challenging recreational experience. This park has trails and views for every experience level, but come prepared to secure permits and do your research to match your expertise.

November 2023

NOTES	SUNDAY	MONDAY	TUESDAY
	5	6	7
			ELECTION DAY (US)
	12	13	14
	FIRST DAY OF DIWALI		
	19	20	21
	26	27	28

November 2023

WEDNESDAY	THURSDAY	FRIDAY	SATURDAY
1 ALL SAINTS' DAY	2	3	4
8	9	10	11 VETERANS DAY (US)
15	16	17	18
22	23 THANKSGIVING DAY (US)	24 NATIVE AMERICAN HERITAGE DAY (US)	25
29	30		

ZION
NATIONAL PARK

LOCATION: Utah

CLIMATE: Summer temperatures can reach sweltering highs of over 110°F, while winters are mild and average temperatures hover between 40°F and 50°F.

BEST TIME TO VISIT: May through October

BIODIVERSITY: 1,000 species of plants, 300 species of birds, 80 species of mammals, as well as fish and reptiles

COMMON WILDLIFE: Plateau lizards, mule deer, wild turkey, rattlesnakes, gray foxes, canyon tree frogs, swifts and western pipistrelles, mountain lions, and porcupines, endangered species, like the California Condor and the threatened Mexican spotted owl

RECREATION: Backpacking, bicycling, camping, horseback riding, canyoneering, rock climbing, swimming, stargazing

NOTABLE ATTRACTIONS: Angels Landing, Observation Point, Emerald Pools, the Narrows, the Subway, Kolob Canyons, Weeping Rock trail, Riverside Walk, Zion Canyon Scenic Drive, Checkerboard Mesa, Zion-Mount Carmel Highway, Human History Museum, Canyon Trail Rides, Crimson Slot Canyon, Bryce Canyon, Peekaboo Slot Canyon

MONDAY (OCTOBER)

30

TUESDAY (OCTOBER) HALLOWEEN

31

WEDNESDAY ALL SAINTS' DAY

1

THURSDAY

2

FRIDAY

3

SATURDAY

4

SUNDAY ◗

5

November 2023

MONDAY 6

TUESDAY ELECTION DAY (US) 7

WEDNESDAY 8

THURSDAY 9

FRIDAY

10

SATURDAY VETERANS DAY (US)

11

SUNDAY FIRST DAY OF DIWALI

12

Be sure to visit the archeological sites throughout Zion to observe evidence of human life dating back 10,000 years.

November 2023

MONDAY ●   **13**

TUESDAY   **14**

WEDNESDAY   **15**

THURSDAY   **16**

FRIDAY

17

SATURDAY

18

SUNDAY

19

Zion's Angels Landing provides spectacular views but should be traversed by experienced hikers only, as it is also dangerous.

November 2023

MONDAY ◖   **20**

TUESDAY   **21**

WEDNESDAY   **22**

THURSDAY THANKSGIVING DAY (US)   **23**

FRIDAY NATIVE AMERICAN HERITAGE DAY (US)

24

SATURDAY

25

SUNDAY

26

The Virgin River runs through Zion and is responsible for carving its stunning canyons.

DECEMBER

Everglades National Park

Known as the only subtropical park in North America, Everglades National Park is a sprawling 1.5 million acres of splendid South Floridian wilderness. While the Everglades may not have elevations that rival other National Parks, such as Glacier or Yellowstone with their towering mountain peaks and daunting hiking trails, this park is not without its scenic vistas. Those that aren't looking for a challenging trek can view the scenery from only a slight rise in elevated vantage point. Trade your hiking boots for a life jacket and take an exhilarating airboat tour through the freshwater marshes to observe, sometimes at high speeds, the vast offerings of observable flora and fauna. Take an up-close look at the largest, protected mangrove forest in the Northern Hemisphere, featuring a rare look at both white and black mangroves. Keep your eyes peeled for magnificent large water birds,

elusive gators, peeping crocodiles, water snakes, turtles, and frogs. As the third largest National Park in the United States, there is no lack of things to do: Grab your poles for some fresh and saltwater fishing, paddle your canoe or kayak through Shark Valley, bring or rent a boat to cruise the scenic waterscapes, or get your feet wet with some slough slogging. There is much to do and learn, so for a deeper look into the park's unique ecosystems, take a number of ranger-led tours featuring discussions on everything from the rich biodiversity of the land and water to the astronomy of the sky. This park calls to birdwatchers and geocachers of all ages, as well as offering ample space to camp, hike, and bike. A true North American treasure, Everglades National Park is a unique gem that can't be missed.

December 2023

NOTES	SUNDAY	MONDAY	TUESDAY
	3	**4** ◗	**5**
	INTERNATIONAL DAY OF PERSONS WITH DISABILITIES		
	10	**11** ●	**12**
	HUMAN RIGHTS DAY		
	17	**18** ◖	**19**
	24	**25** ○	**26**
	CHRISTMAS EVE		BOXING DAY (UK / CAN / AUS / NZ)
	31		
	NEW YEAR'S EVE	CHRISTMAS DAY	FIRST DAY OF KWANZAA

DECEMBER 2023

WEDNESDAY	THURSDAY	FRIDAY	SATURDAY
		1 WORLD AIDS DAY	2
6	7	8	9
13 HANUKKAH (BEGINS AT SUNDOWN)	14	15	16
20	21	22	23
27 WINTER SOLSTICE	28	29	30

EVERGLADES NATIONAL PARK

LOCATION: Florida

CLIMATE: Temperatures range from 63°F to 82°F with rare winter frosts, and an average rainfall of 40 to 65 inches annually, mostly between May and October.

BEST TIME TO VISIT: December through April

BIODIVERSITY: More than 360 species of birds, nearly 300 species of fish, more than 50 species of reptiles, 17 amphibians, and more than 60 species of mammals

COMMON WILDLIFE: Spot rose-hewed spoonbills, red-shouldered Hawks, American alligators and crocodiles, Florida snapping turtles, and 27 different kinds of snakes. Home to endangered mammals, including the Florida panther, the West Indian manatee, and the bottlenose dolphin

RECREATION: Boating, kayaking, and fishing, as well as bicycling, hiking, camping, geocaching, and slough slogging

NOTABLE ATTRACTIONS: Shark Valley's observation tower, Nike Hercules missile base, Florida Bay, Nine Mile Pond, Ten Thousand Islands, Anhinga Trail, Gumbo Limbo Trail, Eco Pond, Snake Bight, Chokoloskee Bay

November/December

MONDAY (NOVEMBER) ○

27

TUESDAY (NOVEMBER)

28

WEDNESDAY (NOVEMBER)

29

THURSDAY (NOVEMBER)

30

FRIDAY WORLD AIDS DAY

1

SATURDAY

2

SUNDAY INTERNATIONAL DAY OF PERSONS WITH DISABILITIES

3

December 2023

MONDAY

4

TUESDAY)

5

WEDNESDAY

6

THURSDAY HANUKKAH (BEGINS AT SUNDOWN)

7

FRIDAY

8

SATURDAY

9

SUNDAY HUMAN RIGHTS DAY

10

On the northern and southern limits, the Everglades hosts both temperate and subtropical species.

DECEMBER 2023

MONDAY

11

TUESDAY ●

12

WEDNESDAY

13

THURSDAY

14

FRIDAY

15

SATURDAY

16

SUNDAY

17

The Everglades is the most prolific breeding ground for tropical wading birds in North America.

December 2023

MONDAY 18

TUESDAY 19

WEDNESDAY 20

THURSDAY WINTER SOLSTICE 21

FRIDAY

22

SATURDAY

23

SUNDAY CHRISTMAS EVE

24

This park houses the largest mangrove ecosystem in the western hemisphere.

December 2023

MONDAY CHRISTMAS DAY
25

TUESDAY BOXING DAY (UK / CAN / AUS / NZ) / FIRST DAY OF KWANZAA ○
26

WEDNESDAY
27

THURSDAY
28

FRIDAY

29

SATURDAY

30

SUNDAY NEW YEAR'S EVE

31

There are nine defined habitats in the Everglades, which are home to 16 endangered or threatened species.

JANUARY
Grand Canyon National Park

Established in 1919, Grand Canyon National Park flaunts a breathtaking 1,218,375 acres of gaping canyons, rushing river tributaries, and dazzling desert landscapes. One of the finest examples of arid erosion in the world, the deep valleys and towering rock formations will stun with their majesty and ancient charm. Dripping in mystery and mysticism, this park contains some of the oldest exposed rock in the world, having been formed over six million years as the Colorado River carved its determined path through the canyon. Spanning 277 miles long and 18 miles wide, there are endless places to explore, so a mule ride through the canyon can help cover ground and offer restful views. Hidden caves scattered throughout the canyon beckon to hikers and explorers of all ages while expert adventurers

answer the call of whitewater rapids and sheer rock walls good for climbing. In an arid, dry climate, visitors will find a wide variety of cacti and desert succulents, and the luckiest travelers will spot yellow, pink, and red vibrantly hued cacti flowers. Teeming with wildlife, keep your eyes open for a large variety of reptiles, fascinating spiders and bugs, bighorn sheep, mule deer, and mountain lions, to name a few. The Grand Canyon offers one of the most visible examples of a worldwide geological phenomenon known as the Great Unconformity, in which 250-million-year-old rock strata lie back-to-back with 1.2-billion-year-old rocks. This park is so enchanting that the Hopi Tribe consider it a gateway to the afterlife.

JANUARY 2024

NOTES	SUNDAY	MONDAY	TUESDAY
....		1 NEW YEAR'S DAY	2 NEW YEAR HOLIDAY (UK-SCT)
....	7	8	9
....	14	15 CIVIL RIGHTS DAY (US) MARTIN LUTHER KING JR. DAY (US)	16
....	21	22	23
....	28	29	30

January 2024

WEDNESDAY	THURSDAY	FRIDAY	SATURDAY
☽ 3	4	5	6
10 ●	11	12	13
◐ 17	18	19	20
24 ○	25	26 AUSTRALIA DAY (AUS)	27 HOLOCAUST REMEMBRANCE DAY
31			

GRAND CANYON NATIONAL PARK

LOCATION: Northern Arizona

CLIMATE: Rainfall averages 21 inches and temperatures can reach well over 100°F in the summer with chilly nights and freezing temperatures in the winter.

BEST TIME TO VISIT: April through June

BIODIVERSITY: 25 species of fish, 50 varieties of reptiles and amphibians, 71 species of mammals, over 300 documented bird varieties, 1,737 known species of plants, 167 species of fungi, 64 varieties of moss, and 195 species of lichen

COMMON WILDLIFE: Desert bighorn sheep, mule deer, mountain lions, coyotes, gray foxes, and a large variety of reptiles, birds, and rodents

RECREATION: Hiking and biking, whitewater rafting and river sports, mule and horseback riding, scenic train rides, camping, helicopter tours, stargazing

NOTABLE ATTRACTIONS: Grand Canyon Skywalk, Mather Point, Trail of Time, Kolb Studio and Hopi House, Desert View Watchtower, Bright Angel Trail, Grandview Point, Hermit's Rest

JANUARY

MONDAY NEW YEAR'S DAY

1

TUESDAY NEW YEAR HOLIDAY (UK-SCT)

2

WEDNESDAY ☽

3

THURSDAY

4

FRIDAY

5

SATURDAY

6

SUNDAY

7

JANUARY 2024

MONDAY 8

TUESDAY 9

WEDNESDAY 10

THURSDAY ● 11

FRIDAY

12

SATURDAY

13

SUNDAY

14

The Grand Canyon is bigger than the entire state of Rhode Island.

January 2024

MONDAY CIVIL RIGHTS DAY (US) / MARTIN LUTHER KING JR. DAY (US)

15

TUESDAY

16

WEDNESDAY ◖

17

THURSDAY

18

FRIDAY

19

SATURDAY

20

SUNDAY

21

With an elevation of over 8,000 feet in some areas, the Grand Canyon can influence weather patterns.

January 2024

MONDAY

22

TUESDAY

23

WEDNESDAY

24

THURSDAY ○

25

FRIDAY AUSTRALIA DAY (AUS)

26

SATURDAY HOLOCAUST REMEMBRANCE DAY

27

SUNDAY

28

There are an estimated 1,000 caves in the park, 335 of which have been recorded. Grab your headlamp!

FEBRUARY
Grand Teton National Park

Grand Teton's dramatic landscape has something for every visitor, with short easy trails for families, wildlife sightings for photographers, and hundreds of mountain trails for the adventurous. The park's towering geological formations and mountains are world-renowned for their beauty and have shaped the imagination of the American West for generations. The dramatic landscapes and geology of Grand Teton National Park lies only 10 miles south of Yellowstone National Park. The Greater Yellowstone Ecosystem, one of the world's largest intact temperate ecosystems, connects these two parks with the scenic J.D. Rockefeller Jr. Memorial Parkway and the surrounding national forests. This is perfect for an extended trip to explore one of the most magnificent landscapes in the lower 48. Take it all in from the top of Signal Mountain, where you can drive to the summit for panoramic views of the whole valley. The iconic sight of the Teton range reflected in

the Snake River is an opportunity not to be missed, and can be seen from a variety of outlooks and landings around the park. The Grand Teton National Park ecosystem is one of the few nearly pristine ecosystems in National Parks holdings, and many of its species have existed there undisturbed since prehistoric times. Due to climate change, some of these species, including the threatened white bark pine, are now managed more fervently to aid in preservation. Humans have been a part of the ecosystem in the region stretching back over 11,000 years, sharing the land with herds of moose, elk, and bison. After the original park was established in 1929, the Shoshone and other Indigenous populations were displaced to the Wind River Reservation to the southeast of the park, where you can learn more about the rich cultural traditions of the valley.

FEBRUARY 2024

NOTES	SUNDAY	MONDAY	TUESDAY
	4	5	6
			WAITANGI DAY OBSERVED (NZ)
	11	12	13
	18	19	20
		PRESIDENTS' DAY (US)	
	25	26	27

FEBRUARY 2024

WEDNESDAY	THURSDAY	FRIDAY	SATURDAY
	1 ◗	2	3
	FIRST DAY OF BLACK HISTORY MONTH	**GROUNDHOG DAY (US / CAN)**	
7	8 ●	9	10
			CHINESE NEW YEAR
14	15 ◖	16	17
VALENTINE'S DAY **ASH WEDNESDAY**			
21	22	23 ○	24
28	29		

GRAND TETON NATIONAL PARK

LOCATION: Wyoming

CLIMATE: The temperature typically varies over the course of the year, from 6°F to 80°F. It is rarely below -13°F or above 87°F, depending on the location in the park.

BEST TIME TO VISIT: May through October

BIODIVERSITY: 1,000 species of vascular plants, 61 species of mammals, 300 species of birds, 24 fish species, and a few species of reptiles and amphibians

COMMON WILDLIFE: Grizzly and black bears, bison, elk, moose, pronghorn, gray wolves, foxes, marten, badgers, otters, osprey, bald eagles, beavers, pelicans, muskrat, marmot

RECREATION: Wildlife watching, hiking, walking, backpacking, camping, mountain climbing, fishing, swimming, boating, and canoeing are available in the summer. Skiing and snowshoeing are available in the winter

NOTABLE ATTRACTIONS: Signal Mountain, Inspiration Point, Hidden Falls, Jackson Hole, Chapel of Transfiguration, Mormon Row Historic District, Jenny Lake, Schwabacher Landing, Snake River Overlook, Oxbow Bend, Taggart, Phelps, and Leigh Lakes, Moose-Wilson Road, Paintbrush Canyon

MONDAY (JANUARY)

29

TUESDAY (JANUARY)

30

WEDNESDAY (JANUARY)

31

THURSDAY FIRST DAY OF BLACK HISTORY MONTH

1

FRIDAY GROUNDHOG DAY (US / CAN)

2

SATURDAY

3

SUNDAY

4

February 2024

MONDAY 5

TUESDAY WAITANGI DAY OBSERVED (NZ) 6

WEDNESDAY 7

THURSDAY 8

FRIDAY ● 9

SATURDAY CHINESE NEW YEAR 10

SUNDAY 11

Book your flight to Jackson Hole Airport, the only airport in a National Park.

February 2024

MONDAY   12

TUESDAY   13

WEDNESDAY VALENTINE'S DAY / ASH WEDNESDAY   14

THURSDAY   15

FRIDAY ◖ **16**

SATURDAY **17**

SUNDAY **18**

The earliest known settlers of Grand Teton were fur trappers, otherwise known as mountain men.

FEBRUARY 2024

MONDAY PRESIDENTS' DAY (US)

19

TUESDAY

20

WEDNESDAY

21

THURSDAY

22

FRIDAY

23

SATURDAY ○

24

SUNDAY

25

Grand Teton is only 10 miles away from Yellowstone. Why not do both?

March
Yosemite National Park

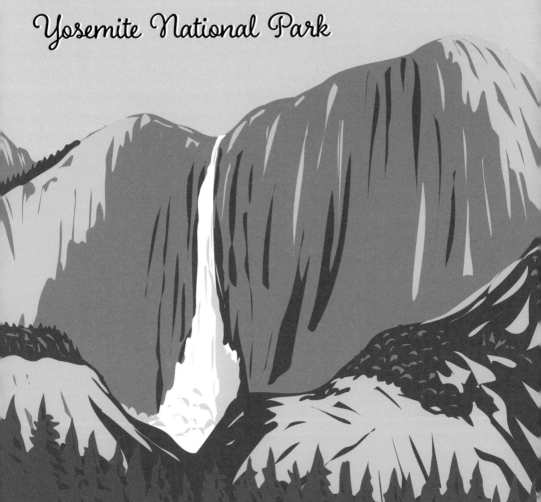

In the Sierra Nevada mountains, the majority of this tranquil and sprawling park is designated wilderness. Plan the perfect itinerary by hiking along one of the 750 miles of trails on foot or horseback. Head to the top of the Merced River Canyon, or the middle of the Tuolumne Meadows with a packed picnic and enjoy simple pleasures while bird watching or fishing. For the wildflower enthusiast, the park's ranging elevation (from 2,000 to 13,000 feet) results in an extremely rich flora environment of 1,450 species. Visit the lower elevations in March to catch the first bloom of tufted poppies and redbuds. By mid-May, if you follow Cook's Meadow Loop to Yosemite Valley, you will witness the California native monkeyflower with its fuchsia, snapdragon-shaped petals that the hummingbirds flock to pollinate. Home to the toughest granite and breathtaking

waterfalls, raft along the Merced River in the summer or strap on your snowshoes for some winter sports in December. Soak up the scenes of Yosemite Valley dressed in sunny meadows of pine and oak, humming with the trembles of falling water. When planning your trip, be sure to head to the southern portion of Yosemite Valley where the Mariposa Grove lives. The largest sequoia grove, it is home to over 500 mature sequoias you'll struggle to wrap your arms around. A few famous, must-visit trees include the Fallen Monarch, the Bachelor, the Three Graces, and the Grizzly Giant. Whether exploring in the fall or spring, you'll be able to say you've visited the "temple of nature," maybe catch some pictures of great gray owls or red foxes, or if you're lucky, an endangered grizzly bear. Just make sure to stay 50 yards away or let the rangers yell and chase them out of the developed areas.

MARCH 2024

NOTES	SUNDAY	MONDAY	TUESDAY
	◗ 3	4	5
	● 10 RAMADAN (BEGINS AT SUNDOWN) MOTHERING SUNDAY (UK)	11 LABOUR DAY (AUS-VIC)	12
	◖ 17 ST. PATRICK'S DAY	18	19 SPRING EQUINOX
	24 PALM SUNDAY	○ 25	26
	31 EASTER		

March 2024

WEDNESDAY	THURSDAY	FRIDAY	SATURDAY
		1 FIRST DAY OF WOMEN'S HISTORY MONTH	2
6	7	8	9
13	14	15	16
20 NOWRUZ	21	22	23 PURIM (BEGINS AT SUNDOWN)
27	28	29 GOOD FRIDAY	30

YOSEMITE NATIONAL PARK

LOCATION: California

CLIMATE: Summers can reach a high of 87°F, and winters, while snowy and cold, can also be both sunny and chilly with lows near 28°F.

BEST TIME TO VISIT: April through October

BIODIVERSITY: Over 262 species of birds, 22 reptiles, 12 amphibians, 90 mammals, and an unknown number of native fish with at least nine non-native fish species

COMMON WILDLIFE: American dippers, great gray owls, Sierra newts, Sierra Mountain snakes, and red foxes. The park's rich habitat is also home to California's endangered species, including grizzly bears, red-legged frogs, and foothill yellow-legged frogs

RECREATION: Hiking, camping, fishing, rock climbing, horseback riding, as well as some water activities and winter sports

NOTABLE ATTRACTIONS: Hetch Hetchy Valley, Glacier Point, Big Trees Lodge, Pioneer Yosemite History Center, Mariposa Grove, Tuolumne Meadows, Yosemite Falls

February/March

MONDAY (FEBRUARY)

26

TUESDAY (FEBRUARY)

27

WEDNESDAY (FEBRUARY)

28

THURSDAY (FEBRUARY)

29

FRIDAY FIRST DAY OF WOMEN'S HISTORY MONTH

1

SATURDAY

2

SUNDAY

3

March 2024

MONDAY 4

TUESDAY 5

WEDNESDAY 6

THURSDAY 7

FRIDAY

8

SATURDAY

9

SUNDAY RAMADAN (BEGINS AT SUNDOWN) / MOTHERING SUNDAY (UK) ●

10

Visit the rock formations at sunset. The granite reflects the sun, causing the rock faces to glow a fiery red.

March 2024

MONDAY LABOUR DAY (AUS-VIC)   11

TUESDAY   12

WEDNESDAY   13

THURSDAY   14

FRIDAY

15

SATURDAY

16

SUNDAY ST. PATRICK'S DAY

17

Reaching up to 2,425 feet, Yosemite Falls is one of the tallest waterfalls in the world.

MARCH 2024

MONDAY 18

TUESDAY SPRING EQUINOX 19

WEDNESDAY NOWRUZ 20

THURSDAY 21

FRIDAY

22

SATURDAY PURIM (BEGINS AT SUNDOWN)

23

SUNDAY PALM SUNDAY

24

The Sierra Nevada red fox was recently spotted in the park on a wildlife cam, the first sighting in 100 years.

MARCH 2024

MONDAY ○   **25**

TUESDAY   **26**

WEDNESDAY   **27**

THURSDAY   **28**

FRIDAY GOOD FRIDAY

29

SATURDAY

30

SUNDAY EASTER

31

In 1932, Yosemite lost a bid to host the Winter Olympic Games to Lake Placid, New York.

APRIL

Joshua Tree National Park

traddling the Colorado Desert and the Mojave Desert in southern California, you'll find 800,000 acres housing ruggedly handsome rocks and a landscape that'll make your mouth run dry—and not just because of the heat. Joshua Tree National Park is a protected region filled with its twisted, bristled namesake, the Joshua tree. Neighbor to some boisterous city centers—Los Angeles, San Diego, Las Vegas, and Phoenix—about 2.8 million visitors wander into its fields to enjoy a true desert excursion each year. For campers, a selection of reservations are available for you to book, including a night spent in the middle of the Cottonwood at 3,000 feet in elevation, where amenities like water, toilets, and fire grates are at your convenience for a weekend away. For those seeking a more adrenaline-inducing activity, take the ranger-led Climber Coffee tour and learn all about rock climbing with complimentary coffee and scenic views you'll crave every

Sunday morning. Joshua Tree has an estimated 8,000 routes for climbing and 2,000 for bouldering, as well as hundreds of gaps for highliners. It's the perfect opportunity to get your fill of a beautiful bird's-eye-view. For those who prefer to keep their feet on the ground, 300 miles of trails for hiking, biking, and birdwatching await you. Mountain bikes and 4-wheel-drive vehicles are also welcome in the park. A geology tour will joggle you across the Covington Flats and along the edge of the Pinto Basin for an off-road adventure by exploring untouched land. After a day of exploration, if you're around on the longest night of the year, the winter solstice, join friends for a relaxing night of stargazing. Come out as early as 4:30 p.m. and settle under a night sky—glittering with stars, planets, and passing meteors—away from city lights. The white-tailed antelope and desert tortoise won't mind

APRIL 2024

NOTES	SUNDAY	MONDAY	TUESDAY
		☽ 1	2
		APRIL FOOLS' DAY	
	7	● 8	9
			EID AL-FITR (BEGINS AT SUNDOWN)
	14	☾ 15	16
	21	22 ○	23
		PASSOVER (BEGINS AT SUNDOWN) EARTH DAY	
	28	29	30

April 2024

WEDNESDAY	THURSDAY	FRIDAY	SATURDAY
3	4	5	6
10	11	12	13
17	18	19	20
24 ADMINISTRATIVE PROFESSIONALS' DAY (US)	25 ANZAC DAY (AUS / NZ)	26	27

JOSHUA TREE NATIONAL PARK

LOCATION: California

CLIMATE: The park's climate is most comfortable in the fall and spring, with highs between 70°F to 85°F and lows around 50°F. In the winter, temperatures range from 60°F to near or below freezing at night. Summers are hot.

BEST TIME TO VISIT: October through May

BIODIVERSITY: Over 250 bird species, two species of amphibians, 46 species of reptiles, and 57 mammals

COMMON WILDLIFE: Roadrunners, phainopeplas, mockingbirds, cactus wrens, white-crowned sparrows, Bendire's thrashers, desert tortoises, white-tailed antelopes, kangaroo rats, California tree frogs

RECREATION: Hiking, camping, stargazing, rock climbing, biking, birdwatching, as well as horseback riding and watching the sunset

NOTABLE ATTRACTIONS: Hidden Valley, Barker Dam, Arch Rock, the Discovery Trail, Indian Cove, Quail Springs, Cap Rock, Cholla Cactus Garden, Keys View, Ryan Mountain, and the wildflowers in the Pinto Basin

APRIL

MONDAY APRIL FOOLS' DAY ◗

1

TUESDAY

2

WEDNESDAY

3

THURSDAY

4

FRIDAY

5

SATURDAY

6

SUNDAY

7

APRIL 2024

MONDAY ●   **8**

TUESDAY EID AL-FITR (BEGINS AT SUNDOWN)   **9**

WEDNESDAY   **10**

THURSDAY   **11**

FRIDAY

12

SATURDAY

13

SUNDAY

14

The Joshua Tree itself isn't a tree; it's actually a yucca plant in the same family as orchids.

MONDAY ◖

15

TUESDAY

16

WEDNESDAY

17

THURSDAY

18

FRIDAY

19

SATURDAY

20

SUNDAY

21

The Joshua Tree was named as such by the Mormons, who sought to honor the biblical Joshua.

APRIL 2024

MONDAY PASSOVER (BEGINS AT SUNDOWN) / EARTH DAY

22

TUESDAY ○

23

WEDNESDAY ADMINISTRATIVE PROFESSIONALS' DAY (US)

24

THURSDAY ANZAC DAY (AUS / NZ)

25

FRIDAY

26

SATURDAY

27

SUNDAY

28

Joshua Tree National Park has three different ecosystems that intersect: the Colorado Desert, the Mohave Desert, and the San Bernardino Mountains.

MAY

Mount Rainier National Park

Are you ready to visit one of the most dangerous volcanoes in the world? It may be quiet right now, but Mount Rainier is an active volcano known to have a high probability of eruption. Also one of the most heavily glaciated peaks in the continental United States, Mount Rainier's landscape is the head of five major rivers and numerous creeks, streams, and waterfalls. More than 20 waterfalls are open to the public, weather conditions permitting. With all this water, conditions may vary greatly depending on the time of year, but the park is still a tempting site to many visitors. Humans have occupied the area for at least 9,000 years, and the park was established in 1899 as the fourth national park in the new National Parks System by President William McKinley. It contains over 25 glaciers actively descending from the peak of the volcano. One of these is the

Carbon Glacier, the largest glacier by volume in the United States. Old growth forest crisscrossed with trails spans the mountain's lower slopes while the upper reaches are covered in seemingly painted wildflower meadows. Its diverse ecosystems are intricate, while fungi play an essential role in their stability. In the shadow of the volcano, visit Paradise, the head of multiple trails including the incredible Skyline Trail. Explore the Carbon River and feel the spray of Narada Falls. Visitors can also pay their respects to the ancient trees in Grove of the Patriarchs, where enormous Douglas firs, red cedars, and western Hemlocks tower over the boardwalk trails. When visiting, make sure to make time for the Mount Rainier Gondola to Crystal Mountain, which offers stunning views and terminates at an atmospheric restaurant.

MAY 2024

NOTES	SUNDAY	MONDAY	TUESDAY
	5	6 ●	7
	CINCO DE MAYO ORTHODOX EASTER	LABOUR DAY (AUS-QLD) EARLY MAY BANK HOLIDAY (UK)	
	12	13	14
	MOTHER'S DAY (US / CAN)		
	19	20	21
		VICTORIA DAY (CAN)	
	26	27	28
		SPRING BANK HOLIDAY (UK) MEMORIAL DAY (US)	

MAY 2024

WEDNESDAY	THURSDAY	FRIDAY	SATURDAY
☽ 1	2	3	4
FIRST DAY OF ASIAN AMERICAN AND PACIFIC ISLANDER HERITAGE MONTH			**YOM HASHOAH (BEGINS AT SUNDOWN)**
8	9	10	11
☾ 15	16	17	18
22 ○	23	24	25
29 ☽	30	31	

MOUNT RAINIER NATIONAL PARK

LOCATION: Washington

CLIMATE: With a combination of forest, subalpine, and alpine environments, this humid climate reaches highs of around 70°F in the summer and lows near 20°F in the winter, with heavy precipitation year-round.

BEST TIME TO VISIT: July through August

BIODIVERSITY: 65 mammal species, 14 species of amphibians, five species of reptiles, 182 species of birds, and 14 species of native fish. Invertebrates likely represent 85% of the animal biomass there, and the park also hosts over 1,000 native plant species

COMMON WILDLIFE: Columbian black-tailed deer, Douglas squirrels, Steller's jays, and ravens

RECREATION: Advanced mountaineering, mushroom foraging, camping and hiking, picnicking, camping, and hiking access, gondola rides, wildflower identification, stargazing

NOTABLE ATTRACTIONS: Paradise recreational area, Lodges at Longmire and Sunrise, Ohanapecosh Hot Springs, Grove of the Patriarchs, and Silver Falls, Carbon River and Carbon River Glacier, Mowich Lake, Myrtle Falls, Reflection Lake, Cayuse Pass and Chinook Pass

MONDAY (APRIL)

29

TUESDAY (APRIL)

30

WEDNESDAY FIRST DAY OF ASIAN AMERICAN AND PACIFIC ISLANDER HERITAGE MONTH

1

THURSDAY

2

FRIDAY

3

SATURDAY YOM HASHOAH (BEGINS AT SUNDOWN)

4

SUNDAY CINCO DE MAYO / ORTHODOX EASTER

5

May 2024

MONDAY LABOUR DAY (AUS-QLD) / EARLY MAY BANK HOLIDAY (UK)

6

TUESDAY ●

7

WEDNESDAY

8

THURSDAY

9

FRIDAY

10

SATURDAY

11

SUNDAY MOTHER'S DAY (US / CAN)

12

Regional Indigenous Peoples called the mountain different variations of the name Tacoma, which means "the source of nourishment from the many streams coming from the slopes."

May 2024

MONDAY 13

TUESDAY 14

WEDNESDAY ◖ 15

THURSDAY 16

FRIDAY

17

SATURDAY

18

SUNDAY

19

Mount Rainier is the most glaciated peak in the United States.

MAY 2024

MONDAY VICTORIA DAY (CAN)　　　　　　　　　　　**20**

TUESDAY　　　　　　　　　　　　　　　　　**21**

WEDNESDAY　　　　　　　　　　　　　　　**22**

THURSDAY ◯　　　　　　　　　　　　　　**23**

FRIDAY

24

SATURDAY

25

SUNDAY

26

Indigenous Tribes of the Mount Rainier region include the Nisqually, Puyallup, Squaxin Island, Muckleshoot, Yakama, and Cowlitz—all maintain relations with the park.

JUNE

Voyageurs National Park

Whether shimmering under the elusive Aurora Borealis in its dark skies or bright Minnesota sun, Voyageurs National Park provides beautiful vistas night and day. Open year-round, its landscape is a series of interconnected waterways that flow northwest as a watershed of the Hudson Bay. In this place of meeting points in the center of North America, humans have made their home for nearly 10,000 years. In the late 1600s, exploration was fueled by the fur trade with local Indigenous populations, including the Ojibwe. While the area was once the focus of industry, with logging, fishing, and the Gold Rush of the nineteenth century, it is now famous for its dark skies and natural beauty, facilitating unmatched stargazing and astrophotography.

Named after the French-Canadian tradesmen who began navigating across its lakes over 250 years ago, almost half the acreage of Voyageurs lies under the waters of the Rainy, Kabetogama, Namakan, and Sand Point lakes. Established in 1975, it is Minnesota's only national park, giving visitors a chance to experience the lakes the way these intrepid travelers did, with fishing, boating, and hiking opportunities abounding. The park is famous for views of the Northern Lights, where there is almost no light pollution. Visitors can hop in a canoe or boat and take over a remote, private island for a night; some islands even have their own trails for hiking to explore this spacious wilderness.

JUNE 2024

NOTES	SUNDAY	MONDAY	TUESDAY
	2	3	4
	9	10	11
	16	17	18
	FATHER'S DAY (US / CAN / UK) 23	24	25
	30		

June 2024

WEDNESDAY	THURSDAY	FRIDAY	SATURDAY
			1
			FIRST DAY OF PRIDE MONTH
5 ●	6	7	8
12	13 ◐	14	15
		FLAG DAY (US)	
19	20 ○	21	22
JUNETEENTH (US)	SUMMER SOLSTICE		
26	27 ◑	28	29

VOYAGEURS NATIONAL PARK

LOCATION: Minnesota

CLIMATE: While summer highs can reach between 70°F and 80°F, winter temperatures drop into the negatives, with averages well below freezing from October to May.

BEST TIME TO VISIT: June through August

BIODIVERSITY: Wildflowers, and wild raspberries, blueberries, and strawberries, hardwood and boreal species of trees, 100 species of birds, 50 species of mammals, and countless amphibians and arthropods

COMMON WILDLIFE: Moose, black bear, beavers, a variety of amphibians, bald eagles, loons, double-breasted owls, warblers, Walleye, Northern pike, lake trout, sturgeon

RECREATION: Fishing, star gazing, as well as boating, canoeing, swimming, hiking and camping in the summer. In the winter, an ice road is opened, with conditions permitting, lake driving on the iced-over lake, snowmobiling, cross-country skiing, ice fishing, and snowshoeing

NOTABLE ATTRACTIONS: Northern Lights, Ellsworth Rock Gardens, Grassy Bay Cliffs, Gold Portage, Kettle Falls, Anderson Bay Overlook, private island camping

May / June

MONDAY (MAY) SPRING BANK HOLIDAY (UK) / MEMORIAL DAY (US)

27

TUESDAY (MAY)

28

WEDNESDAY (MAY)

29

THURSDAY (MAY) 🌓

30

FRIDAY

31

SATURDAY FIRST DAY OF PRIDE MONTH

1

SUNDAY

2

June 2024

MONDAY 3

TUESDAY 4

WEDNESDAY 5

THURSDAY ● 6

FRIDAY

7

SATURDAY

8

SUNDAY

9

The park's name, Voyageurs, is a nod to French-Canadian fur traders who used to frequently travel the area.

June 2024

MONDAY

10

TUESDAY

11

WEDNESDAY

12

THURSDAY

13

FRIDAY FLAG DAY (US) ◖

14

SATURDAY

15

SUNDAY FATHER'S DAY (US / CAN / UK)

16

Grab your poles! The rivers of Voyageurs house many fish, including walleye, smallmouth bass, crappie, and northern pike.

June 2024

MONDAY 17

TUESDAY 18

WEDNESDAY JUNETEENTH (US) 19

THURSDAY SUMMER SOLSTICE 20

FRIDAY ◯

21

SATURDAY

22

SUNDAY

23

Visit Rainy Lake in the winter for some frozen lake driving, snowmobiling, ice fishing, and winter camping.

June 2024

MONDAY 24

TUESDAY 25

WEDNESDAY 26

THURSDAY 27

FRIDAY ◗

28

SATURDAY

29

SUNDAY

30

Camping at Voyageurs requires a boat and reservations.
Hatch a plan!

JULY
Death Valley National Park

Welcome to the hottest, driest, and lowest national park in America. Death Valley is a below-sea-level basin, enduring a steady drought and record summer heat that make it a land of extremes. On your way to the park, the right preparation is required to experience the entrancing scenes of this protected land. In the winter, towering peaks are frosted with snow and then washed away by springtime rain showers, refreshing vast fields of wildflowers. While an unlikely place to live, Death Valley feeds lush oases of fish and wildlife, and remains the home of hard-learned and clever desert animals such as the jackrabbit, bighorn sheep, and numerous thick-skinned reptiles. Established in 1994, and equipped with a ghost town, craters, endangered plant species, and over three million acres of wilderness, it is the largest national park in the contiguous United States. On thousands of miles of both paved and dirt roads, visitors will

discover the beauty and freedom of unhindered wildlife. Glimpse the stunning scenic views on the hills of Artists Palette, where colors from volcanic deposits are splashed and vibrant. Go down to the lowest point at 282 feet below sea level in Badwater Basin, where you can walk across a landscape of salt flats composed of sodium chloride, calcite, gypsum, and borax. Or see it from a higher vantage point with a half-day trip to Dantes View for an unparalleled perspective 5,000 feet above. For those wanderers looking for a longer escape into the wild, take the route to the Wildrose charcoal kilns, where you'll stumble upon the ten beehive structures created for mining operations in the late 1800s. Whether you're looking to backpack through the backcountry, picnic on the dunes, or bring your van for camping, a well-prepared traveler will receive a lifetime's worth of soaking up the sights, sounds, and smells of nature at Death Valley.

July 2024

NOTES	SUNDAY	MONDAY	TUESDAY
		1 CANADA DAY (CAN)	2
	7	8	9
	14	15	16
○	21	22	23
	28	29	30

JULY 2024

WEDNESDAY	THURSDAY	FRIDAY	SATURDAY
3	4 ●	5	6
	INDEPENDENCE DAY (US)		
10	11	12 ◖	13
17	18	19	20
24	25	26 ◗	27
31			

DEATH VALLEY
NATIONAL PARK

LOCATION: California and Nevada

CLIMATE: Summer temperatures often reach 120°F. Winter and spring are very pleasant, but winter storms and summer monsoons can bring rain, and spring commonly has dust storms.

BEST TIME TO VISIT: October through May

BIODIVERSITY: Nearly 400 bird species, six fish species, five amphibians, 36 reptiles, and 56 mammals

COMMON WILDLIFE: Bighorn sheep, kangaroo rats, desert tortoise, coyotes, jackrabbits, roadrunners, bats, gophers, foxes, badgers, mountain lions, reptiles, and others that can operate in the heat and don't have to worry about dehydration

RECREATION: Hiking, camping, backcountry driving, backpacking, road and mountain biking, jogging, trailrunning, sightseeing, and stargazing

NOTABLE ATTRACTIONS: Dante's View, Desolation Canyon, Golden Canyon, Mesquite Flat Sand Dunes, Zabriskie Point, Badwater Basin, Harmony Borax Works, Ubehebe Crater, Dark Sky Festival. Also, visit the place where the famous *Star Wars* movie series filmed scenes in the park for Tatooine in *Episodes IV* and *V*

JULY

MONDAY CANADA DAY (CAN)

1

TUESDAY

2

WEDNESDAY

3

THURSDAY INDEPENDENCE DAY (US)

4

FRIDAY ●

5

SATURDAY

6

SUNDAY

7

July 2024

MONDAY 8

TUESDAY 9

WEDNESDAY 10

THURSDAY 11

FRIDAY

12

SATURDAY 🌓

13

SUNDAY

14

When the sand slides off the high dunes, it creates a scraping sound similar to a voice or pipe organ. Singing sand dunes? Join the chorus!

July 2024

MONDAY 15

TUESDAY 16

WEDNESDAY 17

THURSDAY 18

FRIDAY

19

SATURDAY

20

SUNDAY ○

21

Visit Racetrack Playa, where the rocks move on their own and leave trails across the terrain tracing their paths.

July 2024

MONDAY

22

TUESDAY

23

WEDNESDAY

24

THURSDAY

25

FRIDAY

26

SATURDAY ☽

27

SUNDAY

28

There are hundreds of birds in Death Valley, but the most famous is the roadrunner. Beep beep!

August

Acadia National Park

Once the summer escape of Hudson Valley artists, "rusticators," and the wealthy east coast elite and their estates, the islands and coastline of Acadia National Park were eventually protected as a national monument by President Woodrow Wilson in 1916. The park's status was formalized in 1929. Acadia's lands are home human history dating back 10,000 years, most notably with the Indigenous Peoples of the Wabanaki Confederacy. The landscape of the park includes a heavily glaciered coast and islands with a wide range of biodiverse habitats. It also includes Cadillac Mountain, the tallest peak on the Atlantic Coast. The park preserves more than half of Mount Desert Island, part of the Isle au Haut on the tip of the Schoodic Peninsula, as well as its surrounding areas. This stunning coastline features Somes Sound, the only fjord on the East Coast. Once you arrive at the sprawling park, visit Bar Harbor and explore the scenic town, enjoy the beach, or delve deeper into the park and hike some of the 150 miles of trail. You can also bike or walk on

the beautifully maintained historical carriage roads that span some of the most scenic areas of the park. Come in the winter and enjoy a winter wonderland draped in pristine white snow. Acadia is open year-round, although certain areas are subject to closures due to snowfall or flooding, so do some homework before planning your trip. Rangers lead tours from May to October, allowing visitors to delve into the park's deep natural and cultural history. The dark sky areas of the park are also popular, with the Acadia Night Sky Festival attracting writers, speakers, scientists, and other luminaries as well as tourists. Interest in the park has increased dramatically in the past few years, and the park remains one of the country's top ten most visited national parks. Come prepared for crowds in the summer, but the park is quieter for scenic fall foliage and green springs for those willing to venture off the beaten path.

August 2024

NOTES	SUNDAY	MONDAY	TUESDAY
	● 4	5	6
		SUMMER BANK HOLIDAY (UK-SCT)	
	11 ◗	12	13
	18 ○	19	20
	25 ◗	26	27
		SUMMER BANK HOLIDAY (UK-ENG / NIR / WAL)	

AUGUST 2024

WEDNESDAY	THURSDAY	FRIDAY	SATURDAY
	1	2	3
7	8	9	10
14	15	16	17
21	22	23	24
28	29	30	31

ACADIA NATIONAL PARK

LOCATION: Maine

CLIMATE: Summers are warm, humid, and mild, with highs around 70°F, and winters are cold with average temperatures below freezing, around 20°F.

BEST TIME TO VISIT: May through October

BIODIVERSITY: 40 species of mammals, over 300 species of birds, and 30 species of fish, in addition to reptiles, amphibians, and invertebrates. It is also home to a vast array of marine wildlife in the tidepools, coastal areas, and open ocean

COMMON WILDLIFE: Falcons, owls, eagles, loons, ducks and shorebirds, beavers, foxes, deer, snails, mussels, crabs, lobsters, seals, whales, porpoises

RECREATION: In the summer, drive the park loop road by bus or car, hiking, as well as bicycling, horseback riding, fishing, swimming, kayaking, and guided boat tours. Winter activities include cross-country skiing, snowshoeing, snowmobiling, and ice fishing

NOTABLE ATTRACTIONS: Bar Harbor, Cadillac Mountain hiking and peak drive, Mount Desert Island, Thunder Hole, Jordan Pond House, Sand Beach and Echo Lake, Blackwoods Campground, Drive Park Loop

JULY/AUGUST

MONDAY (JULY)

29

TUESDAY (JULY)

30

WEDNESDAY (JULY)

31

THURSDAY

1

FRIDAY

2

SATURDAY

3

SUNDAY ●

4

AUGUST 2024

MONDAY SUMMER BANK HOLIDAY (UK-SCT)

5

TUESDAY

6

WEDNESDAY

7

THURSDAY

8

FRIDAY

9

SATURDAY

10

SUNDAY

11

Barack Obama was the first US president to visit Acadia National Park on vacation.

AUGUST 2024

MONDAY ☽   12

TUESDAY   13

WEDNESDAY   14

THURSDAY   15

FRIDAY

16

SATURDAY

17

SUNDAY

18

Acadia was named after the Arcadia region of Greece because some claim the landscapes look similar.

AUGUST 2024

MONDAY ○   19

TUESDAY   20

WEDNESDAY   21

THURSDAY   22

FRIDAY

23

SATURDAY

24

SUNDAY

25

Acadia's weather can switch from cold to hot to rainy in a heartbeat, so bring your jacket, umbrella, and sunscreen!

SEPTEMBER
Mammoth Cave National Park

On your next trip to Kentucky's Cave Country, gather the whole family for an exciting, otherworldly visit to Mammoth Cave National Park. Known for the world's longest cave of over 400 miles, the grandeur of this cavernous experience is incomparable. Rich in human history and biodiversity, both on the surface and under, across 53,000 acres of land, these ecosystems are home to species from the white-tailed deer to eyeless fish that live in the deepest, darkest recesses of the caves. Dedicated in 1941, it earned the title of UNESCO World Heritage Site in 1981 and an International Biosphere Reserve in 1990. With over 30 miles of the Green and Nolin Rivers, jump in a canoe, kayak, or boat for some water recreation. When planning your river trip, as long as you wear a life jacket and check the weather forecast beforehand, you'll have access to boating and water sports such as paddling, sailing, diving, snorkeling, and more. The cave

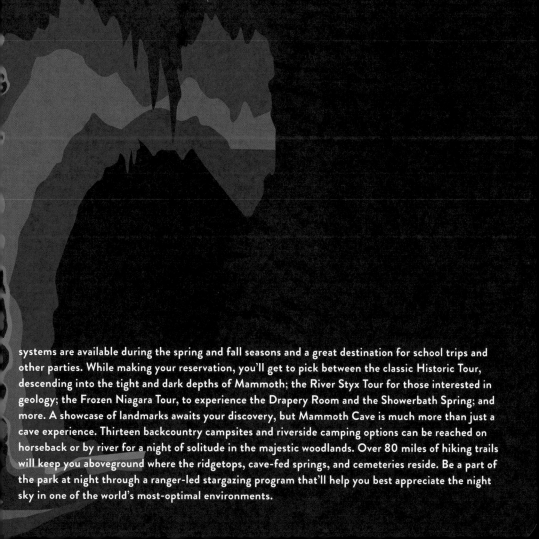

systems are available during the spring and fall seasons and a great destination for school trips and other parties. While making your reservation, you'll get to pick between the classic Historic Tour, descending into the tight and dark depths of Mammoth; the River Styx Tour for those interested in geology; the Frozen Niagara Tour, to experience the Drapery Room and the Showerbath Spring; and more. A showcase of landmarks awaits your discovery, but Mammoth Cave is much more than just a cave experience. Thirteen backcountry campsites and riverside camping options can be reached on horseback or by river for a night of solitude in the majestic woodlands. Over 80 miles of hiking trails will keep you aboveground where the ridgetops, cave-fed springs, and cemeteries reside. Be a part of the park at night through a ranger-led stargazing program that'll help you best appreciate the night sky in one of the world's most-optimal environments.

SEPTEMBER 2024

NOTES	SUNDAY	MONDAY	TUESDAY
	1 ●	2	3
	FATHER'S DAY (AUS / NZ)	LABOR DAY (US) LABOUR DAY (CAN)	
	8	9	10
	GRANDPARENTS' DAY (US)		
	15	16 ○	17
	FIRST DAY OF NATIONAL HISPANIC HERITAGE MONTH		
	22	23 ◗	24
	FALL EQUINOX		
	29	30	

SEPTEMBER 2024

WEDNESDAY	THURSDAY	FRIDAY	SATURDAY
4	5	6	7
11	12	13	14
PATRIOT DAY (US)			
18	19	20	21
25	26	27	28

MAMMOTH CAVE
NATIONAL PARK

LOCATION: Kentucky

CLIMATE: Summer temperatures can exceed 90°F with high humidity, but the temperature in the cave stays in the mid-50s. Afternoon thunderstorms are common.

BEST TIME TO VISIT: June through August

BIODIVERSITY: Over 50 species of mussels and a few species of turtles on the river, as well as birds, and large and small mammals on the surface. More than 160 species inhabit the cave system, including over 70 species that are threatened, or endangered

COMMON WILDLIFE: Eastern gray squirrels, salamanders, wild turkey, white-tailed deer, Allegheny woodrats, Rafinesque's big-eared bats, cave fish, and crayfish

RECREATION: Cave tours, camping, scenic drives, canoeing, kayaking or boating, fishing, hiking, bicycling, horseback riding, and stargazing

NOTABLE ATTRACTIONS: Mammoth Cave Railroad steam engine and train car, Mammoth Cave Baptist Church & Cemetery, Good Spring Baptist Church & Cemetery, Doyel Valley Overlook, Sunset Point, Turnhold Bend Overlook, Green River Bluffs Overlook, Green River Valley, Heritage Trail, Echo River Spring Trailhead

AUGUST/SEPTEMBER

MONDAY (AUGUST) SUMMER BANK HOLIDAY (UK-ENG / NIR / WAL) ◗ **26**

TUESDAY (AUGUST) **27**

WEDNESDAY (AUGUST) **28**

THURSDAY (AUGUST) **29**

FRIDAY (AUGUST) **30**

SATURDAY (AUGUST) **31**

SUNDAY FATHER'S DAY (AUS / NZ) **1**

September 2024

MONDAY LABOR DAY (US) / LABOUR DAY (CAN) ●

2

TUESDAY

3

WEDNESDAY

4

THURSDAY

5

FRIDAY

6

SATURDAY

7

SUNDAY GRANDPARENTS' DAY (US)

8

Mammoth Cave's dome reaches 192 feet high, while its Bottomless Pit sinks 105 feet deep.

SEPTEMBER 2024

MONDAY 9

TUESDAY 10

WEDNESDAY PATRIOT DAY (US) (11

THURSDAY 12

FRIDAY

13

SATURDAY

14

SUNDAY FIRST DAY OF NATIONAL HISPANIC HERITAGE MONTH

15

This park's oldest caves are over 10 million years old and are the world's longest-known cave system.

September 2024

MONDAY   16

TUESDAY ◯   17

WEDNESDAY   18

THURSDAY   19

FRIDAY

20

SATURDAY

21

SUNDAY FALL EQUINOX

22

The cave shrimp found in Mammoth Cave are found nowhere else on Earth and are now an endangered species.

September 2024

MONDAY   23

TUESDAY ◗   24

WEDNESDAY   25

THURSDAY   26

FRIDAY

27

SATURDAY

28

SUNDAY

29

People have been visiting Mammoth Cave for over 125 years, and it is considered one of the new Seven Wonders of the World.

OCTOBER
Redwood National Park

Known for some of the tallest and oldest trees on Earth, this park protects a vast area of wide-ranging ecosystems, including prairies, woodlands, rivers, and coastline. Visitors have always been awed by this resilient landscape, where prescribed fires are part of the ecosystem's management, and the trees tower far above everything else. With scenic drives that span the length of the park and a wide array of camping opportunities, it's a place to get in touch with these majestic trees, their careening heights, and their impossibly wide girths. There's even an opportunity to drive straight through one of these massive giants—the Chandelier Drive-Thru Tree. Today this park and its adjacent linked parks protect almost half of the state's remaining coastal redwoods. In the early 19th century, the redwoods spanned more than 2,000,000 acres, and logging decimated the population of these enormous specimens by nearly 95 percent. Efforts toward conservation began in 1920, culminating with the park's establishment in 1968. It has also been designated as a UNESCO World Cultural Site and International Biosphere Reserve.

Indigenous Peoples have occupied and utilized the park landscape, and some still live in the park today.

The redwood tree's sheer enormity has captured visitors' imaginations as long as they've traveled to the region. The largest living redwood in the park, named Hyperion, is also the world's tallest tree, and stands nearly 380 feet tall. These majestic trees are highly resistant to disease and can support whole ecosystems on their massive limbs, where plants and animals thrive more than 150 feet above the ground, functioning as keystone guardian species of these remarkable forests, and their preservation is vital to all that live there. Pay homage to these venerable giants at the magnificent Stout Grove, where old-growth redwoods thrive. You can even explore the famous Fern Canyon, which made an appearance in the *Jurassic Park* franchise. If you plan ahead, you can even camp out on Gold Bluffs Beach to watch the sun set over the Pacific Ocean as you rest from a long day in

OCTOBER 2024

NOTES	SUNDAY	MONDAY	TUESDAY
			1
	6	7	8
		LABOUR DAY (AUS-ACT / NSW / SA)	
	13	14	15
		INDIGENOUS PEOPLES' DAY (US) COLUMBUS DAY (US) THANKSGIVING DAY (CAN)	
	20	21	22
	27	28	29
		LABOUR DAY (NZ)	

OCTOBER 2024

WEDNESDAY	THURSDAY	FRIDAY	SATURDAY
● 2	3	4	5
ROSH HASHANAH (BEGINS AT SUNDOWN)			
9	● 10	11	12
		YOM KIPPUR (BEGINS AT SUNDOWN)	
16 ○	17	18	19
SUKKOT (BEGINS AT SUNDOWN)			
23 ◗	24	25	26
	SIMCHAT TORAH (BEGINS AT SUNDOWN)		
30	31		
	FIRST DAY OF DIWALI HALLOWEEN		

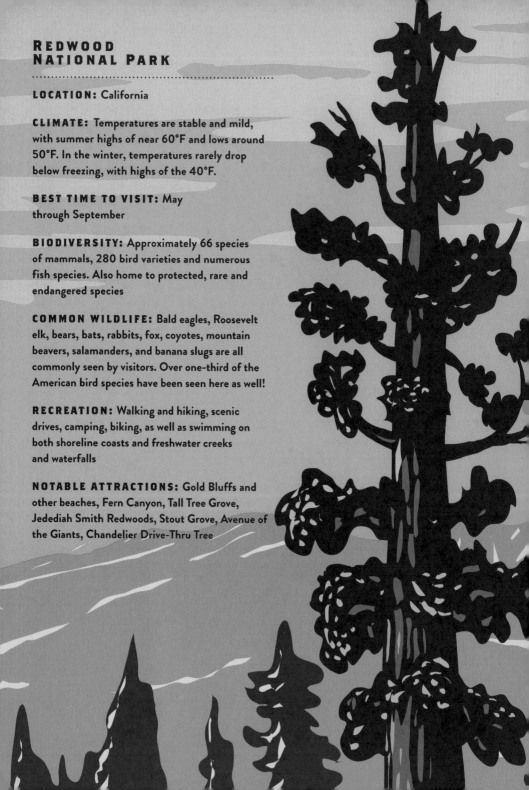

REDWOOD NATIONAL PARK

LOCATION: California

CLIMATE: Temperatures are stable and mild, with summer highs of near 60°F and lows around 50°F. In the winter, temperatures rarely drop below freezing, with highs of the 40°F.

BEST TIME TO VISIT: May through September

BIODIVERSITY: Approximately 66 species of mammals, 280 bird varieties and numerous fish species. Also home to protected, rare and endangered species

COMMON WILDLIFE: Bald eagles, Roosevelt elk, bears, bats, rabbits, fox, coyotes, mountain beavers, salamanders, and banana slugs are all commonly seen by visitors. Over one-third of the American bird species have been seen here as well!

RECREATION: Walking and hiking, scenic drives, camping, biking, as well as swimming on both shoreline coasts and freshwater creeks and waterfalls

NOTABLE ATTRACTIONS: Gold Bluffs and other beaches, Fern Canyon, Tall Tree Grove, Jedediah Smith Redwoods, Stout Grove, Avenue of the Giants, Chandelier Drive-Thru Tree

SEPTEMBER/OCTOBER

MONDAY (SEPTEMBER)

30

TUESDAY

1

WEDNESDAY ROSH HASHANAH (BEGINS AT SUNDOWN) ●

2

THURSDAY

3

FRIDAY

4

SATURDAY

5

SUNDAY

6

OCTOBER 2024

MONDAY LABOUR DAY (AUS-ACT / NSW / SA)

7

TUESDAY

8

WEDNESDAY

9

THURSDAY

10

FRIDAY YOM KIPPUR (BEGINS AT SUNDOWN)

11

SATURDAY

12

SUNDAY

13

Redwoods are the tallest trees on Earth, with some reaching over 300 feet high.

October 2024

MONDAY INDIGENOUS PEOPLES' DAY (US) / COLUMBUS DAY (US) / THANKSGIVING DAY (CAN)

14

TUESDAY

15

WEDNESDAY SUKKOT (BEGINS AT SUNDOWN)

16

THURSDAY ○

17

FRIDAY

18

SATURDAY

19

SUNDAY

20

Some creatures, such as the wandering salamander, live their whole lives in the canopy of the trees.

October 2024

MONDAY 21

TUESDAY 22

WEDNESDAY 23

THURSDAY SIMCHAT TORAH (BEGINS AT SUNDOWN) ◗ 24

FRIDAY 25

SATURDAY 26

SUNDAY 27

Redwoods are climate-change heroes, capturing more carbon dioxide than any other tree on Earth.

November

Hawai'i Volcanoes National Park

In search of island adventure? The many volcanoes found at Hawai'i Volcanoes Park are active enough that there are new, observable eruptions happening every day, though visitors are not always allowed close enough to observe active lava flows. Two of the world's most active volcanoes, Kīlauea and Mauna Loa are located in this park, which are also held as sacred sites by the native Hawaiians. In the past, the surrounding area was used for cattle grazing, ranching, and industry, but was established as a natural park in 1916 by President Woodrow Wilson. This can be a volatile area, as the park was recently closed due to intense volcanic activity in 2018. It has since reopened to the public, but some areas are intermittently closed for safety, so double check accessible areas before planning your trip. Both main volcanoes are currently active, with the most recent eruptions occurring in 2020. It's important to obey signs and notices of trail closures, as they are there to keep visitors safe. Even still, there are opportunities to observe activity if you're

lucky—rangers can offer guided hikes and active lava flows can be seen via helicopter tour (plan to observe around or after sunset for best effect).

Designated an International Biosphere in 1980 and UNESCO World Heritage Site in 1987, the park's shifting geology and new formations are a huge draw to tourists, who have been coming to the islands for recreation since the 1840s. Visitors can even drive along a chain of previous volcanic craters that was once buried in a 1969 eruption. Recently, the park acquired a new area of over 16,000 acres, which includes portions of the Ala Kahakai National Historic Trail and a variety of important historical and cultural sites, as well as a portion of critical coastline habitat, home to many endangered, threatened, or rare species. The park's span is home to many trails that allow visitors to explore previous lava flows and archeological sites, hike along an old portion of a crater, and even walk through a rainforest cave where a river of lava long ago flowed.

November 2024

NOTES	SUNDAY	MONDAY	TUESDAY
		3	4	5
				ELECTION DAY (US)
	10	11	12
		VETERANS DAY (US)	
	17	18	19
	24	25	26

November 2024

WEDNESDAY	THURSDAY	FRIDAY	SATURDAY
		● 1	2
		ALL SAINTS' DAY	
6	7	8 ◐	9
13	14 ○	15	16
20	21 ◑	22	23
27	28	29	30
	THANKSGIVING DAY (US)	NATIVE AMERICAN HERITAGE DAY (US)	

HAWAI'I VOLCANOES NATIONAL PARK

LOCATION: Hawai'i

CLIMATE: With year-round temperatures between 60°F and 70°F, the temperature rarely tops 80°F, nor does it drop below 35°F.

BEST TIME TO VISIT: November through March

BIODIVERSITY: While the recent park expansion means species cataloging is still underway, most native species of the park are those that were able to fly, float, swim, or otherwise drift their way to the islands. Native species are often threatened or endangered, including 23 surviving endemic Hawaiian songbirds, while a number of invasive species thrive.

COMMON WILDLIFE: Kalij pheasants, wild pigs, goats, coqui frogs, wildcats, mongoose, Hawaiian hoary bats, native nēnē geese, 'Io hawks, tropical and sea birds, and aquatic life such as sea turtles, humpback whales, Hawaiian monk seals, 'opihi limpets, dolphins, tropical fish

NOTABLE ATTRACTIONS: Crater Rim Trail or Keanakāko'i Crater, the Pu'uloa Petroglyphs, the Ha'akulamanu Sulphur Banks, Nāhuku Thurston Lava, Chain of Craters Road, Devastation Trail, Hōlei Sea Arch

MONDAY (OCTOBER) LABOUR DAY (NZ)

28

TUESDAY (OCTOBER)

29

WEDNESDAY (OCTOBER)

30

THURSDAY (OCTOBER) FIRST DAY OF DIWALI / HALLOWEEN

31

FRIDAY ALL SAINTS' DAY ●

1

SATURDAY

2

SUNDAY

3

November 2024

MONDAY | 4

TUESDAY ELECTION DAY (US) | 5

WEDNESDAY | 6

THURSDAY | 7

FRIDAY

8

SATURDAY ☽

9

SUNDAY

10

According to locals, Hawai'i Volcanoes is home to Pele, the goddess of volcanoes and fire and creator of the Hawaiian Islands.

November 2024

MONDAY VETERANS DAY (US)

11

TUESDAY

12

WEDNESDAY

13

THURSDAY

14

FRIDAY ○   15

SATURDAY   16

SUNDAY   17

Out of all the Hawaiian Islands, the Big Island is the youngest, having been created by eruptions of six of the park's volcanoes.

November 2024

MONDAY

18

TUESDAY

19

WEDNESDAY

20

THURSDAY

21

Mauna Kea Volcano reaches 13,796 feet above sea level, while its depths reach around 19,700 feet below sea level.

DECEMBER
Virgin Islands National Park

While the Virgin Islands are known as a beautiful tropical destination for relaxation, they are also a stunning and biodiverse haven for nature. The Virgin Islands National Park covers two-thirds of the island of St. John and has over 3,000 years of human history in addition to gorgeous natural scenery. This park is an opportunity to engage with the island's challenging history of sugar plantations. Offering visitors stunning white sand beaches, swimming, diving colorful coral reefs, boating, and camping, the Virgin Islands Park is an incredible place to experience the Caribbean ecosystem at your own pace. Opportunities also exist to help support sea turtles by signing up to observe and document nesting as a citizen scientist. Visitors can also explore the park's marine ecosystems, as over 40 percent of the park is underwater. With dense mangrove-lined shorelines, seagrass beds, and numerous coral formations, you can find world-class snorkeling and easy-access dives. Or simply relax on the gorgeous beaches preserved for both native species and visitors alike.

Explore the park by land for stunning views and a chance to see parts of the Caribbean that aren't easily accessible from more resort-focused locations. Arm yourself with plenty of water and sunscreen and strike out to discover special private alcoves to swim. Keep your eyes peeled for fascinating early plantation ruins and ancient rock carvings by the Indigenous Taíno people. Visit the single sacred baobab tree brought to the island by formerly enslaved Africans. Soak in the scent of bay rum trees, once the island's claim to fame. The rewards for such explorations are vistas of the island and sea, and trails range widely from leisurely strolls to strenuous hikes, not to mention its rich and sometimes troubling history.

DECEMBER 2024

NOTES	SUNDAY	MONDAY	TUESDAY
	● 1	2	3
	WORLD AIDS DAY		INTERNATIONAL DAY OF PERSONS WITH DISABILITIES
	◐ 8	9	10
			HUMAN RIGHTS DAY
	○ 15	16	17
	◗ 22	23	24
			CHRISTMAS EVE
	29	● 30	31
			NEW YEAR'S EVE

December 2024

WEDNESDAY	THURSDAY	FRIDAY	SATURDAY
4	5	6	7
11	12	13	14
18	19	20	21 WINTER SOLSTICE
25 CHRISTMAS DAY HANUKKAH (BEGINS AT SUNDOWN)	26 BOXING DAY (UK / CAN / AUS / NZ) FIRST DAY OF KWANZAA	27	28

VIRGIN ISLANDS NATIONAL PARK

LOCATION: US Virgin Islands

CLIMATE: The tropical park experiences minimal variation in temperature between summer and winter, with an average temperature of 79°F.

BEST TIME TO VISIT: November through April

BIODIVERSITY: 140 species of birds, 302 species of fish, seven species of amphibians, 22 species of mammals, and 740 species of plants, as well as over 50 species of coral and other sea life, both as permanent occupants and additional transitory/migrating marine life

COMMON WILDLIFE: Sea turtles, coral, lizards, a wide variety of migratory birds, deer, goats, sheep, donkeys, cats, mongoose, pigs

RECREATION: Snorkeling, boating, paddle boarding, kayaking and diving, hiking, camping

NOTABLE ATTRACTIONS: Underwater Snorkel Trail, Trunk Bay, beaches of Cinnamon Bay, sea turtles at Maho Bay, birding at Francis Bay boardwalk, Coral Reef National Monument

November/December

MONDAY (NOVEMBER)

25

TUESDAY (NOVEMBER)

26

WEDNESDAY (NOVEMBER)

27

THURSDAY (NOVEMBER) THANKSGIVING DAY (US)

28

FRIDAY (NOVEMBER) NATIVE AMERICAN HERITAGE DAY (US)

29

SATURDAY (NOVEMBER)

30

SUNDAY WORLD AIDS DAY ●

1

December 2024

MONDAY

2

TUESDAY INTERNATIONAL DAY OF PERSONS WITH DISABILITIES

3

WEDNESDAY

4

THURSDAY

5

FRIDAY

6

SATURDAY

7

SUNDAY ☽

8

Visit Trunk Bay with its underground tunnel of coral reefs. Be gentle; the coral is becoming damaged from overuse.

December 2024

MONDAY

9

TUESDAY HUMAN RIGHTS DAY

10

WEDNESDAY

11

THURSDAY

12